T0384324

Raising Tiny Humans

From Potty Training to Prejudice,
A Survival Guide for the Wild
Toddler Years and Beyond

Written and Illustrated by
Liz Swenson

FAMILIUS

One of the most difficult and persistent struggles of parenting is that your job is CONSTANTLY changing. Like once you feel like you are finally getting sleep and feeding down, you start needing to introduce solids. Now you are worried about choking and which foods are best. Once you hit your stride there, you are dealing with a newly independent tiny human with insatiable curiosity and a taste for danger. And then, one day, it is your job to raise kind, tolerant, and loving little humans that will be big humans in the blink of an eye. This guidebook is my humble attempt to hold your hand during this crazy journey you have embarked on—to give you all my best tips and tricks, to help you raise your perfectly unique little human in the way that is best for your family and our world. I have every confidence that you are up to the task and your tiny human will thrive and make this world a better place. I hope this little guidebook will help you find your way.

AND THEN THE
ADVENTURE GETS TRICKY...

Welcome
to the
jungle

Axl Rose

Okay, first off, you are doing great. You are absolutely nailing the parenting thing, and your baby has thrived and survived their first crazy year. Not to freak you out, but your job is about to get a lot more complex and intense. Like, keeping-your-composure-when-you-get-slapped-in-the-face-by-your-toddler-in-the-middle-of-a-grocery-store, intense. Yeah, I know. But I also know you are up to this crazy task. Turns out that sweet little baby is actually a tiny human and that tiny human is craving more and more independence by the minute. Raising these amazing little beings will be the joy of your life, and also, at times, an exhausting frustration. Like all great adventures, this one will require you to face challenges you never expected, to get lost and then found again, and, most of all, to grow personally. It's a wild ride, but you totally got this!

Xoxxoo,
Liz

Contents

Getting lost is easy, and it happens often. Even though I don't always have all the answers, and I don't always know what to do, I do have this handy dandy compass that helps me find my way. Loving, Connecting, Gardening, or Growing—one of these cardinal points always gets me back on track—even in my most desperate and confounding moments.

Compass dial text: Love, Garden, Connect, Grow

LOVE YOUR WORLD
LOVE YOUR COMMUNITY
LOVE YOUR PEOPLE
LOVE YOUR CHILD
LOVE YOUR PARTNER
LOVE YOURSELF

It all starts here, and it is all built on this. This is first. Always.

4

Focusing first on connection produces children who are not only happier, but easier.

Dr. Laura Markham

CONNECT

PARENTING LIKE A GARDENER

GARDEN

Here's what I mean by grow:

Are you the adult you want your child to grow up to be?

Brené Brown

I know—it's super juicy, but you got this!!

GROW

Body

Spoiler alert: Sleep will just never be the same once you have kids, and potty training does not end your experience with their excrement. As you watch your toddler grow into a kid, expect food protests, huge swings in appetite, and more energy than you ever thought humanly possible at six in the morning. It's absolutely mind blowing to see how capable they become in just a few short years. And yet, all of that really is small potatoes to what I believe is your most important job: making them feel good in their skin—helping them grow confidence inside and out. It's a wild ride, but you totally got this.

ACTUAL PHOTO OF ME
CHANGING MY TODDLER'S DIAPER

Veggies build strong bodies!

Did you know gorillas are mostly vegan?

Eat

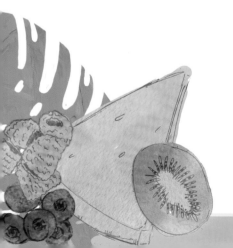

EAT
THE
RAINBOW

Red and pink fruits and vegetables help your heart and eyes stay healthy and strong.

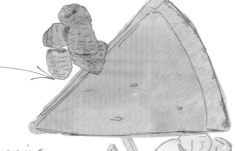

Orange and yellow fruits and veggies give your body super powers to fight off germs and heal cuts.

Green fruits and veggies protect your brain and eyes.

Blue and purple veggies and fruit can help you learn and protect your cells.

18

Trust
(their)
~~your~~
gut.

The less restrictive wording we use with kids, the better they will be able to figure out how to read their own body cues.

Emily Lauren Dick
Author of *Body Positive*

Explore!

Trying new foods together is fun! And it's a great way to model openness and facing fears.

Cookie Ball Recipe

1 cup pitted dates

1 cup almonds

1 cup unsweetened shredded coconut.

Blend the dates and almonds in a food processor until smooth. Roll the almond/date paste into 2-inch balls. Roll the balls in a shallow dish filled with shredded coconut. Refrigerate and serve as a sweet treat or snack.

Cut into pieces or flatten as needed for your child.

Tons of plant-based protein and vitamins for a big upgrade to a typical "sweet treat."

There are lots of ways to
make fruits and veggies fun:

*Put fruit on a stick and freeze it for
a summer treat.

*Make a silly face or animal with their
veggies.

*Let them cook with you.

*Have them make art with their veggies.

*Give healthy foods fun names like
"Hulk Muffins," "Superhero sprouts,"
and "Unicorn Horns" for carrots.

PLAY WITH YOUR FOOD

The sooner that veggie get's from the ground to your mouth, the more nutrients it has.

Visiting a farmers market with your kiddo is a great way to get them excited about veggies and more connected with their food.

Vegan, full of spinach, and my kids' favorite.

Hulk Muffins Recipe

Dry ingredients:

1½ cup whole wheat flour

½ cup oat flour

1½ tsp cinnamon

2 tsp baking powder

½ tsp baking soda

¼ tsp salt

Wet ingredients:

¾ cup hemp or oat milk

⅓ cup agave

3 large ripe bananas

6 oz spinach

½ cup melted vegan butter or vegetable oil

1 flax egg

1 tsp vanilla extract

Combine dry ingredients in a large bowl, mix with a fork until combined. Blend all the wet ingredients in a blender. Pour blended wet ingedients into dry ingredients. Combine and bake at 350° for 20-25 minutes. Check with a toothpick. When it comes up clean, they are done. Makes 18-20 muffins.

Yes, they really are this green.

AWAKE-ISH

Sleep

(The thing you thought you would get once you were out of the baby-phase)

Probably the most essential component of getting your kids (and yourself) a good night's sleep.

Bedtime Routine

Here is our current bedtime routine. It has changed and adapted as my kiddos have grown, but our magic formula of: bath + reading + gratitudes + song + hugs and kisses has remained the same.

Good night

READ FOR 20 MINUTES

TAKEN A BATH

BRUSHED YOUR TEETH

LAID OUT TOMORROW'S OUTFIT

PUT ON PJS

GONE POTTY

TIME FOR GRATITUDES, SNUGGLES, GOODNIGHT HUGS AND KISSES!

I LOVE YOU! SLEEP WELL MY LOVES!

30

Sleeping with your toddler is like sleeping with a drunk octopus looking for its keys.

Ahhhh you've put your toddler to bed now you can finally —just kidding he's up again.

Simon Holland

Your life will forever change once your toddler escapes their crib.

*If you want your toddler sleeping in their own bed, here's what I've got:

Basically every single time they come out of their room, you walk them back to bed, kiss their head, tuck them in, and don't engage. Don't chat, don't get them the water they are asking for, just quietly return them to bed, and that is it.

This could very possibly be about 100 times the first night, then 50 the second, then 15 the next, and then they normally get it by then, and you won't have any big issues.

*Like all things relating to sleep and children, expect disruptions during growth spurts, sickness, nightmares, and every third Tuesday. You have children, you just aren't going to get that sleep you want for a loooong time.

34

Today me will live in the moment, unless it's unpleasant in which case me will eat a cookie.

Cookie Monster

36

Let the adventure begin!

Potty Training 101

Step #1

Make Sure They are Ready

Studies have shown if you push kids into potty training too early, it actually takes longer for them to master.

SIGNS OF POTTY-TRAINING-READINESS
(Most children show readiness between 18 and 24 months)

Physical

* Can walk.

* Can pull pants up and down on their own.

* Pulls at dirty diapers.

* Dry for two-hour increments (or dry when they wake up from a nap).

Emotional

* Talks about going potty (before or after they go).

* They seem interested in pottying, watching or imitating when you go.

* Can follow basic instructions.

Time to gear up!

Step #2
Make Sure You are Ready

Are you moving?

Just had a new baby?

Starting a new school?

then... NO PE

You want to wait for a relatively calm moment in your life to try potty training.

42

Step #3

Throw a Potty Party

Wooohoo! Spoiler—it's not a super fun party. Also, it's a three day long party.

This party takes place in your home for three consecutive days. It's very similar to a lock down.

Don't give up if day one is hard. Normally by day two they really start figuring it out!

44

HOW TO THROW A POTTY PARTY

Gear up

* Kids book on potty training.

* Potty chair.

* Undies (about 20 pairs).

* Cleaning supplies.

* Sweet treat (like raisins or jelly beans).

Hype it Up

* Start talking about the big potty event coming up.

* Take them shopping for their undies.

* Read potty books.

* Talk about being a big kid.

* Make them feel like this is special.

The more exciting, silly, and fun you make this experience, the better!

Potty Party Time

Have three days worth of fun indoor activities planned.

*

Give them lots of fluids.

*

Look for the "potty wiggles" and get them to the potty as quickly as you can.

*

At regular intervals ask if they are dry, but don't take them to the potty in regular intervals (you're trying to get them to recognize those potty feelings).

*

If you catch them mid-accident, pick them up and take them to the potty as quickly as you can so they can finish there.

*

Celebrate every success (potty in the potty) with a ridiculous amount of enthusiasm and a sweet treat.

Repeat for two more days.

46

Yup, one minute you think you have it all figured out the next, you don't. It's a long process, and that is ok.

Potty training comes and goes in phases, and setbacks often occur; the most valuable lesson is to be patient and listen to your child's cues.

Dr. Dina DiMaggio

Pediatrician at Pediatric Associates of NYC

Top tips for surviving potty training

* Lower your expectations. This is a process, and it's not a very fun process.

* You will be doing lots of clean up and lots of laundry.

* Never reprimand for accidents. They are doing their best and feeling like they are "in trouble" will make everything harder.

* Bring backup clothes every time you leave the house.

* Night time potty training does not have to be done at the same time.

* Butt-wiping is a whole other skill that will take your kiddo a while to learn, and until they figure it out, it's your job.

Nighttime dryness is a completely different developmental process.

Dr. Natale, MD, Pediatrician

NIGHTTIME POTTY TRAINING

Ok here's what I've got:

It just doesn't work until their body is ready.

Try to have them empty their bladder twice before bedtime.

Practice an enormous amount of patience.

Mom! Can you come wipe my butt?

ALL DAY EVERY DAY

52

Let's do this!

OCTONAUTS

This is a good life goal.

Are you and your children physically active enough to break a sweat each day?

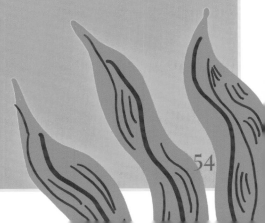

54

How much physical activity should my kids be getting each day?

3-5 YEARS

Take your toddler on walks around the neighborhood or let them have outdoor free play.

Need at least 3 hours of physical activity per day, or about 15 minutes every hour they are awake.

Preschoolers are ready for catching, throwing, and kicking balls. They should get at least 1 hour of a sweat-inducing activity.

6 AND OLDER

Need 60 minutes of moderate to vigorous physical activity on most days of the week.

Elementary students can have fun with organized sports and free play.

What a good day to
be proud of all the
progress I've made.

Building Body Confidence in Kids

If we want our children to love and accept who they are, our job is to love and accept who *we* are.

Brené Brown

Read inclusive books with diverse characters: ones that look like them, ones that don't.

Simple ways to teach body love and confidence every day:

1. Model it and make sure never to criticize your body in front of them.

2. Avoid complimenting physical appearance and instead focus on the inside:

"I love how brave you are!"

"Look at my strong confident kiddo!"

3. Teach them to listen and respect their bodies:

"Eat until you feel full."

"That cookie tasted great! How did it make you feel?"

"You have a tummy ache? Maybe you could take a break from drinking the rest of your juice until you feel better."

4. Teach them their body is their buddy that they get to take care of:

"How is your body feeling today?"

"What can you do to make your body feel better right now?"

"Looks like your body wants to get those wiggles out."

~~pretty~~   strong

~~cute~~   kind

~~skinny~~   hard-working

~~tall~~   creative

~~handsome~~   funny

~~beautiful~~   brave

~~short~~   happy

OUTSIDE-IN VS. INSIDE-OUT

Outside-in:

"When someone tells me I'm pretty, it makes me feel good inside."

Inside-out

"My kindness and determination make me beautiful."

How cool would it be if our kids were in charge of how beautiful they felt.

I get to be me if I belong, I have to be like you to fit in.

Brené Brown

When you love your kiddo without conditions and accept them as they are, you let them know they belong in your family.

Love the skin you're in.

Beautiful me!

(ACTIVITY)

Help children pick crayons or colored pencils that accurately show their skin, hair, and eye color, and draw themselves. Ask, "What makes you, you?" Around their drawing, help children write:

• Descriptions of their racial, ethnic, and cultural identity, for example: African American, Black, biracial, Cherokee, Japanese American, Irish American, Jewish, Muslim, Puerto Rican, White.

• Words that describe their skin color.

• Traditions and heritage, including places their families call "home."

• Finally, write about what makes them special.

FIND THIS ACTIVITY AND MANY MORE AT WWW.SESAMESTREETINCOMMUNITIES.ORG

Mommy, why do people
have different skin colors?

Melanin

Melanin is something that we each have inside our bodies that gives us our skin, hair, and eye color.

Because we all have different amounts and types of melanin, we each have different skin, hair, and eye color.

Having more of certain types of melanin can make skin darker or hair more red.

Everyone's skin, hair, and eyes are a unique combination of certain types and amounts of melanin.

Which is why everyone is so unique and beautiful.

68

SEE (AND LOVE)
THE RAINBOW.

THREE SPECTRA OF GENDER

Biological Sex

FEMALE ⟷ MALE

The physical sex characteristics a
child is born with and develops.

Gender Identity

GIRL ⟷ BOY

How a child, in their head, defines
their gender, based on their
understanding of gender norms.

Gender Expression

GIRL ⟷ BOY

The way a child presents gender,
through their actions, dress, and
demeanor.

Sarah was born a girl, feels like a girl inside, and detests all things "girly."

Bella was born a girl, but she never really felt like she was a girl, and she didn't feel like a boy either. The pronoun "they/them" makes them feel more comfortable, and they prefer to go by the name Max. Sometimes Max dresses in a more feminine style, and other times they prefer a more masculine look.

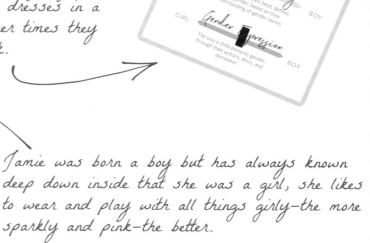

Jamie was born a boy but has always known deep down inside that she was a girl, she likes to wear and play with all things girly—the more sparkly and pink—the better.

You are you and that's super cool.

When my kids are frustrated, defeated, and want to give up, I tell them to repeat after me:

I am smart.

I am loved.

I am strong.

I am unique.

I can do hard things.

I can be anything.

Learning to
grow with
the flow—
you know?

Behavior

When our first baby started throwing tantrums, making demands, and acting aggressive, we mostly just did what our parents did: time-outs, consequences for negative behaviors, and it all worked pretty well. When we tried these traditional parenting strategies with our second child, everything got worse. She refused to stay in place for time-outs, consequences never mattered, and everything would escalate really quickly. I felt very helpless. I was venting to my aunt about how nothing I was doing was working and she said as casually as can be, "Well, why don't you try something else?" And so we did. We basically started treating our children like we treat each other. We asked if something was going on if they acted out. We reassured them that we loved them in moments when they were clearly tired, overwhelmed, and emotional. It was a huge shift for us, and I wish we had done it sooner. There are still plenty of big feelings in our home, but those are now mostly met with empathy and long talks about how we can do things better next time. As you navigate the emotionally challenging job of raising so-called-well-behaved children, remember that each child is unique, and so is your family. You will find your own way and really can't go wrong if love and connection are at the center.

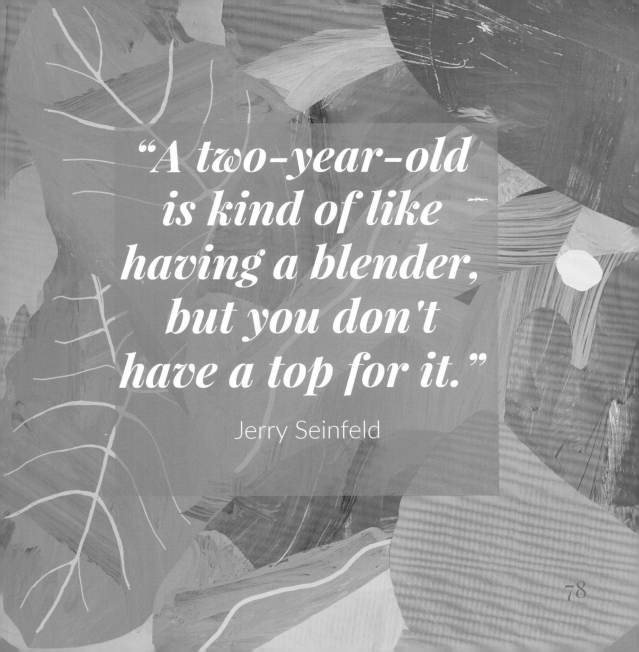

"*A two-year-old is kind of like having a blender, but you don't have a top for it.*"

Jerry Seinfeld

DANCE PARTY

My favorite way to lighten the mood, connect with my kids, and get through tasks I hate—like, dishes, folding laundry, and helping the kids clean their room.

Keeping the Peace

Did you know toddlers are physiologically obsessed with power?

(So a situation like this is actually a sign of healthy brain development, even though, it is actually, super annoying.)

How to ruin a toddlers day:

1. Ask what they want for breakfast.

2. Make exactly that.

CHOICES = POWER

Shhh...
(so give them arbitrary choices, and they will feel like they are getting power.)

ARBITRARY CHOICES YOU CAN GIVE ALL DAY LONG:

It's time to go. Do you want to wear your dinosaur shoes or your red ones?

It's time for bed. Do you want to wear your tiger pjs or your choo choo train pjs?

We're leaving. Do you want to buckle or do you want mommy to buckle?

Role-Playing
(NOT LIKE THAT.)

Role-playing the outcome you want (like going to school, going to bed, or visiting grandma) with dolls and toys is a really effective way to calm an anxious kiddo—especially if you include silliness and giggles.

GIGGLING GARNERS CONNECTION AND STRESS RELIEF.

Kids release emotions in two ways: laughter and crying. So if you get them giggling, there will probably be less crying: win-win!

CONNECTED KIDS ARE BETTER BEHAVED KIDS.

Snuggle fights.
(AKA PILLOW FIGHTS)

A super fun way for kids to release stress and feel connected. Try to have a snuggle fight every day.

Special Time.

15 minutes each day playing with them, doing whatever they want to do.

Do Something You Like To Do (with them)

Paint, bake, play piano, go to museums, a musical, or Sephora. It doesn't matter, just include them in something you enjoy.

Share a Story.

Share a time you have struggled with something they are struggling with. "Hey Bud, I didn't like avocados when I was little either, but I kept trying them, and now they are one of my favorite foods."

When you are with your kiddo, try to be engaged. Put away the devices, make eye contact, let your face light up with the love you have inside for them.

Pay at ten tion

Here is a morning routine that my family uses. I have made this into a sign and placed it by my kids room to help them remember and stay on track.

ROUTINES
ROUTINES
ROUTINES

When kids know what to expect, they feel more in control, and you can expect better behavior. The routines themselves aren't as important as the consistency with which they are implemented.

Good morning

TIME TO:

MAKE-BED

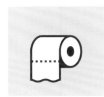

GO POTTY

EAT BREAKFAST

BRUSH TEETH

BRUSH HAIR/WASH FACE

GET DRESSED

PUT ON SHOES

PUT YOUR LUNCH IN
YOUR BACKPACK

GRAB A WATER

YOU ARE GOOD TO GO!!
LOVE YOU!

DISTRACTIONS PYRAMID

PLAY THE SONG "WHAT DOES THE FOX SAY?" BY YLVIS

EYE SPY AND SPOT THE DIFFERENCE

CRAYONS AND COLORING BOOKS

SNACKS

In case of emergency.

Crap! You forgot snacks and crayons!

You are in good shape if you remember these

Always bring snacks!

WHEN YOU FORGET THE DISTRACTIONS:

EYE SPY:

"I spy with my little eye something green and shaped like a triangle or starting with the letter S."
Kids love this game and will keep it going forever!

SPOT THE DIFFERENCE :

This game is very helpful if you are sitting at a table waiting for food. Have your kiddo look at the table and ask them what they see. Then hold up a napkin or have them close their eyes and change the place of a few things, then ask them if they can spot the difference.

INSTEAD OF THIS :

TRY THIS:

"Five more minutes."

"Three more slides."

Kids don't understand time, so they feel really ambushed when you give them amounts of time until "go time." Expect a tantrum at "go time" if you are giving a time to leave.

MARCO!
POLO!

This is our family go-to. Kids can wander off, and this is a way to easily find them in a low-stress way. We practice at home, and then, if I ever lose sight of them when we are out and about, I yell, "Marco!" and they always yell, "Polo!" and we can find each other quickly.

96

BOUNDARIES

WITH

empathy.

LIMITS

WITH

love.

This is basically it. Decide what you are and are not ok with, set the limit, and when they inevitably become upset about it, offer love and understanding. "It's hard when we don't get to do what we want, but it's important for mommy to keep you safe, and so you can't play with knives."

You are the best parent you can be when you love and care for yourself.

I'm going to keep repeating this because you're going to need constant reminding.

Take a break.

Never underestimate the power of nature! Get outside in nature to calm a fussy toddler, kid, or parent.

TANTRUMS
=
Big Feelings

↑

Re-framing helps you empathize. Everytime you see a tantrum, think, "Oh! My kiddo is having some big feelings. How can I help them calm down?"

Tantrums

ANATOMY OF A TANTRUM

Prefrontal Cortex
Takes a long time to develop and helps with impulse control, processing information, and logic.

Amygdala
Detects a threat and sends a warning to the hypothalamus.

Will throw the body into, "Fight or Flight, when deemed necessary.

Hypothalamus
In charge of our involuntary body functions like breathing, heart rate and digestion.

Completely offline, cannot regulate emotions and does not understand language.

FIGHT!!!!!

Increased heart rate, rapid breathing, screaming, flailing limbs.

DADDY HAS GIVEN ME THE WRONG COLOR SPOON!!!

HOW TO STAY

Calllm:

Connection *Every moment is an opportunity to connect.*

Acceptance *This moment is happening and that's ok.*

Love *Remember the first moment you held this baby? Let your heart fill up with that love.*

Listen *What are they trying to tell you right now? What do they need?*

List *Are they hungry? Tired? Stressed out by a move or new school?*

Magic *Your own special magic that is unique to you.*

Feelings are ok.

There's no single trick, or five step process to managing a tantrum because no two tantrums are alike. There will be times when your kiddo wants space, and times when they need a hug. Times they might try to hit you, and times when they will try to hit themselves. There will be times when they are so upset there's no way for them to process verbal communication, and others when you can catch it before they explode and can help them calm down. Each tantrum/meltdown will be unique, and, as the parent, it's your super-fun job to stay calm and safely help them to come out of their fight-or-flight-animal state and back to their tiny-human state. Here's what I have to get through these moments and (try) to make them an experience of real connection where they learn the boundaries of the family and learn not to be ashamed or afraid of their emotions

GEARING UP FOR A TANTRUM

In any challenge being prepared will give you an advantage. Tantrums are no different. The right mindset and a good set of gear can make all the difference.

TANTRUM SURVIVAL PACK

Find a safe, quiet place.

Nature.

↑

The more the better. Petting an animal, looking at a flower, going outside.

If they are reacting to a boundary, repeat that the boundary is still there, but you understand why it upsets them.

Stay CALLLM.

This is soooo much easier said than done, but, if you lose control, then none of this other stuff will be doable.

Offer a hug.

Offer space but say, "I'm here for you."

Sing a song to
calm them down.
*"Henry is sad and
wants to play, oh how
I love Henry today."*

*Name and validate the feelings.
"I get it, that's frustrating when
your toy doesn't work."*

Empathy

More empathy

*Validate the magnitude of the
feelings. "I bet that feels as
big as this house."*

Say, "I love you.
I'm here for you
always, and I'm
not going
anywhere."

Share a story
of when you
were upset
and calmed
down.

Be the boundary.

"I will not let you hit me." (Hold arms.)

Belly breaths,
blowing bubbles,
1-2-3 breaths.

CALMING BREATHS TO PRACTICE WITH YOUR LITTLE:

Belly Breaths

Put your hands on your belly. Imagine you have a balloon in your belly. When you breathe in the balloon gets bigger, as you breathe out the balloon gets smaller. Breathe in through your nose, fill the balloon, breathe out, flatten the balloon.

Take a deep breath in like you are smelling a beautiful flower. Breathe in, breathe out, ahhhhhhhhh.

1-2-3 Breaths

Deep breath in through your nose (count 1-2-3) and then let it out through your mouth with an audible… ahhhhhhhhh

Take an imaginary bubble wand
and blow the biggest bubble.

Simplify, slow down, be kind. And don't forget to have art in your life—music, paintings, theater, dance, and sunsets.

Eric Carle

MORE CALMING STRATEGIES:

Animal Alphabet:

Ask your child to make up a list of animals using the ABCs. For example, they might start with, "Alligator, Bear, Cow, Donkey, Elephant..."

Story of the Day:

Have your child think about the very beginning of the day. Ask, "What was the very first thing you did when you woke up?" Then, have her say the very next thing she did. Then the next, and the next.

WHEN YOU ARE *ABOUT* TO LOSE IT:

Intentionally close your mouth, breathe in through your nose, and stop talking.

Whatever they did to set you off, let it go for the moment.

Take three deep breaths, and even a few push-ups will help your brain come down from fight-or-flight.

Remember to stay Calllm.

"You are not the boss of me," I whisper to myself as I put on his blanket the "right way."

Scary Mommy

Lost your temper?

Turns out you're human. Tell your kids that you are sorry. Tell them why. Then focus on what you can learn, and don't beat yourself up.

Do the best you can until you know better. Then when you know better, do better.

Maya Angelou

NAVIGATING A TANTRUM IN THE WILD

1. Yes, everyone is looking at you (your child is screaming at full volume—that's attention grabbing). Let's pretend for the sake of your sanity that they are not thinking, "Oh look, a terrible parent," and instead imagine they are cheering you on thinking, "Ugh been there, good luck girl, you're doing great!"

2. Remove your kiddo from the situation. "I'm going to pick you up and take you to a safer place right now."

3. Focus on safety. (Don't hit themselves or you) "I won't let you hit."

4. Look through that survival pack, empathy and a hug are generally a winning combo.

5. See if they are calm enough to return to the situation. If not, leave the situation.

Willful children
make dynamic adults.

Sometimes it's easy to get lost in the day-to-day and forget that the feistiness that is making this moment hard for you will eventually serve this child, and the world, very very well.

When you see a flame

keep it lit.

Michelle Obama

The feeling is
okay,
the behavior is
not.

Aggression

124

Consequences should be:

1. Implemented immediately.

2. Related to the behavior.

For example:

" I will not let you hit your sister with your dinosaur. I'm taking the dinosaur to keep everyone safe."

BE THE BOUNDARY

There are times (lots of them actually) when you will need to restrain your child. Hold their arms or legs and say, "My job is to keep you and your sister safe, I will not let you hit her."

Why are they acting the way they are acting?

Be a detective.

What are they feeling?

What skill are they struggling with?

If we want to cultivate worthiness in our children, we need to make sure they know that they belong and that their belonging is unconditional.

Brené Brown

It's especially important to let them know they still belong when they have done a bad thing.

time-in

/tīmˈin/

noun

A method of interrupting a bad behavior or big emotion before they escalate by removing the child from the situation and bringing them to a calmer area. During a time-in the caregiver will help the child calm down, offering empathy and curiosity for the cause of the behavior or emotions.

"Time-ins were a game changer in our household."

That's what happens.

LINDSAY MARIANI

Letting natural consequences take their course is a really valuable teaching tool. It's hard to watch, but it's good for the

YOU ARE BAD.

VS

You did a bad thing.

So small, yet so impactful. Separate your child from the behavior, and they learn they are not bad, the behavior is.

ON SIBLING FIGHTS:

1. Step in between them and be the boundary.

2. Take a deep breath.

3. If one of them is hurt, comfort that child and enlist the aggressor to help by grabbing a bandaid or water.

4. Sit with them both and breathe until they are calm enough to talk.

5. Take turns having each child explain what happened.

6. Help your kiddos listen to each other. "What did you hear your sister say?" "How do you think they are feeling?"

7. Make a plan together to avoid this conflict in the future.

If your child is bitten, kicked, or hit, it can trigger intense emotions caused by

FIGHT
OR
FLIGHT

Even if the perpetrator is your three year old.

BE A COMPASSIONATE SPECTATOR INSTEAD OF REFEREE:

"I see that you're upset that your sister is using your paper. It's hard when you both want to play with the same thing. I think you two can figure this out."

You're big enough, you're big enough, to think of what to do.

Daniel Tiger's Parents

This little song is suuuper helpful for me and the kids. It teaches them empowerment, responsibility, and even conflict resolution. It teaches me to let go and let them figure things out their own way.

136

Make no mistake, the world needs ALL types of children. The quiet, easy-going peacekeepers that sit still and observe, the loud, shake it up, feel it deep, changemakers that are always on the go and every unique soul in between.

Angela Pruess LMFT

Better together.

A lot of
patience,
a lot of
communication,
a lot of
respect.

It is important to note here that all this connection and empathy is impossible if you do not take time for yourself. You must take time to fill your cup.

You know in your gut which is glass and which is plastic. Honor that.

Brain

144

The growth and development of a child's brain is mesmerizing and spectacular to witness. Watching them start to verbalize will fill your heart with a kind of awe that is indescribable, and you might find yourself excitedly describing their every accomplishment to anyone who will listen. I watched over the course of two years my child learn a completely new language—it's bonkers! So how do we help this process along? The good news is that our children learn like a flower blooms, it just happens with incredible beauty and ease. The other good news? There's tons of research out there on how to optimize this learning experience. I've synthesized what I think are the most important ideas for creating a nourishing soil for your little bud to bloom.

every single day

READ

As often as you can.

By the age of two, children who are read to regularly display greater language comprehension, larger vocabularies, and higher cognitive skills than their peers.

ABCDEFG
HIJKLMN
OPQRSTU
VWXYZ

Singing the ABCs activates both sides of a child's brain and helps to lay the foundation for reading.

Learning to Read

Word family sorting with blocks.

Just write some simple word families on building blocks and let them sort.

Flash card hide and seek.

Hide 10-15 flash cards and have them sound out the word, letter, or number when they find it.

My kids loved these games!

Spell out small words in sand.

Play word games in the car:

"What rhymes with pan?" "What sound does dog start with?" "What sound does cat end with?"

I read you read.

Sometimes kids can get nervous about reading and will avoid it. This was our favorite trick to get our little one reading.

Whatever you do:

Make it fun!

Children become more creative simply by playing. They also build their linguistic, cognitive, visual spatial, social, and emotional skills.

Pamela Li

PLAY = LEARNING = PLAY = LEARNING = PLAY = LEARNING =

152

Playing in the grass, collecting crunchy leaves, and playing with hummus and other squishy colorful foods are all examples of sensory play.

sensory play

/ˈsensərē plā /

noun

1. Any activity that uses the senses of touch, taste, smell, sight, hearing, movement, and balance.

"Did you know sensory play builds nerve connections in the brain and even supports language development?"

Embrace the mess.

Getting dirty reduces stress, strengthens sensory synapses, and boosts your child's immune system.

You will be shocked by how entertained your children will be with trash.

"Passive toys make active learners"

Magda Gerber

Finger painting in an empty bathtub.

(It's the best)

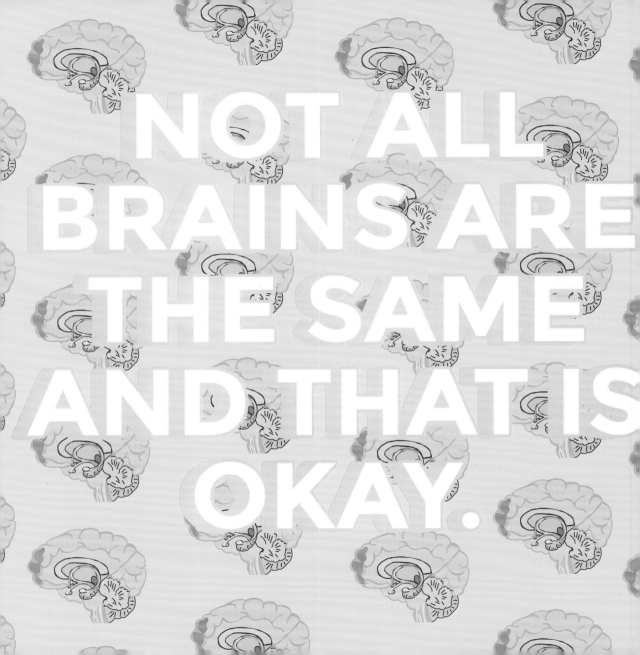

NOT ALL BRAINS ARE THE SAME AND THAT IS OKAY.

1 in 44

Eight-year-old children have been identified as having autism spectrum disorder (ASD).

Trust your gut and talk to your doctor if you have concerns with your child's behavior or development. There are many benefits to early detection.

18 to 24

Months is when ALL children are recommended to be screened for ASD.

Boys are

4 times

more likely to be diagnosed with ASD than girls.

*American Academy of Pediatrics

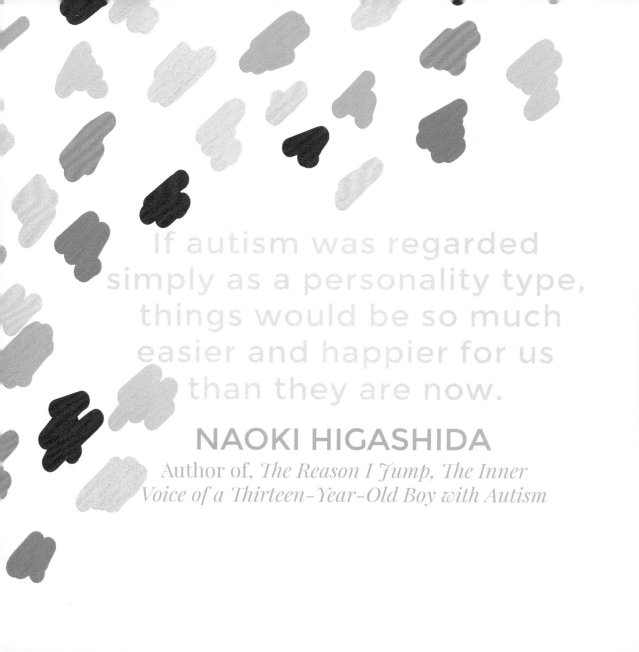

If autism was regarded simply as a personality type, things would be so much easier and happier for us than they are now.

NAOKI HIGASHIDA

Author of, *The Reason I Jump, The Inner Voice of a Thirteen-Year-Old Boy with Autism*

With the simple act of recognizing all brains are unique and not necessarily functioning as our own, we open ourselves to a wider view in which we can empathize and communicate more fully.

growth mindset

/grōTH ˈmīn(d)set/

noun

1. The belief that all abilities can be developed through dedication and hardwork.

"In a growth mindset, challenges are exciting rather than threatening. So rather than thinking, oh, I'm going to reveal my weaknesses, you say, wow, here's a chance to grow." —Carol Dweck

I can do hard things

162

PRAISE THE PROCESS

INSTEAD OF THIS :

"You are so smart!"

TRY THIS:

"I love how hard you are working at that."

This isn't always easy, but keep working at it. Just like them, you are working to get better.

All things are difficult before they are easy.

"I don't know, but let's figure it out together."

This models that it is okay not to know the answer right away and that it is fun to figure things out.

THE POWER

OF

yet

Yet is one of the more powerful tools you can use to garner growth-mentality in your child.

I can't do this *yet*.

I'm not good at this *yet*.

I don't get it *yet*.

It doesn't make sense *yet*.

executive function

/igˈzekyədiv ˈfəNG(k)SH(ə)n /

noun

1.A set of mental skills that include working memory, flexible thinking, and self-control.

 "Trouble with executive function can make it hard to focus, follow directions, and handle emotions, among other things."

Understood.org

The brain needs this skill set to filter distractions, prioritize tasks, set and achieve goals, and control impulses.

Center on the Developing Child
Harvard University

ACTIVITIES THAT DEVELOP EF (EXECUTIVE FUNCTION) SKILLS BY AGE:

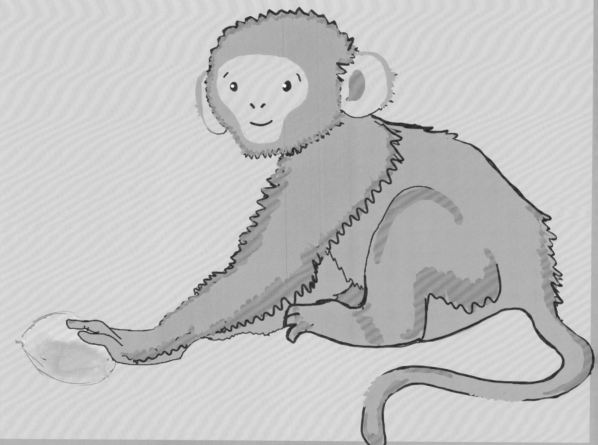

18-36 MONTHS

Active play:

*Trying any new skills

*Itsy Bitsy Spider

*Hokey Pokey

*Head Shoulders Knees and Toes

*Freeze dance

*Ring Around the Rosie

Conversation play:

*Watch and narrate their play. "Is the tiger eating some breakfast?"

*Tell stories about shared events. "Remember when we went to visit grandma and you played with the Mr. Potato Head?"

*See and label a child's feelings: "It looks like you are mad that we have to leave the park."

Sorting play:

*Sort objects by size or color.

*Silly sorting: big objects in a small bucket, small items in a big bucket

*Simple puzzles

Imagination Play:

*Toddlers often imitate adult actions. Encourage this by asking them questions about what they are doing, and narrate what you are seeing.

*Play along as they pretend.

172

*Activities recommended by the Center on the Developing Child Harvard University

3-5 YEARS

Active play:

*Get them to the park! (Or any place where they can challenge themselves physically.)

*Set up obstacle courses and games that encourage complex motions like skipping or jumping on one foot.

*Freeze dance with extra challenges, like freezing into specific positions or dancing really fast and really slow.

*Sing songs that repeat and add on, like "She'll Be Coming 'Round the Mountain."

*Sing the Alphabet song.

Conversation play:

*Tell group stories. One child starts the story, and each person adds something to it.

*Have your children tell you a story, write it down, and have them act it out later. It can be revisited and changed as they like.

Quiet play:

*Matching games with more complicated rules or "Opposites Bingo" so they mark "day" if "night" is called out

*Increasingly complicated puzzles

*Cooking

Imagination Play:

*Support high level imaginary play by reading books and going on field trips, so they know enough about the scenarios they are acting out.

*Provide varied props, toys , play food, or dress up. You could also let them use their imaginations and make their own play props.

*Activities recommended by the Center on the Developing Child Harvard University

5-7 YEARS

Active play:

*Musical Chairs

*Red Light, Green Light

*Duck, Duck, Goose

*Four Square

*Dodgeball

*Simon Says

*Soccer

*Yoga

*Tae Kwon Do

Card & Board Games:

*Go Fish

*Old Maid

*Crazy Eights

*Uno

*Spoons

*Slapjack

*Snap

*Concentration
(Uncover cards to reveal matches.)

Quiet play:

*Puzzle and brain teaser books with mazes and simple word finds

*Logic and reasoning games like Chess or Traffic Jam

*20 Questions

*I Spy

174

*Activities recommended by the Center on the Developing Child Harvard University

Break down tasks:

(A great way to help build EF skills.)

CLEAN YOUR ROOM

First, let's:

PUT BOOKS ON BOOK SHELF

Now, let's:

THROW LAUNDRY IN HAMPER

PUT AWAY STUFFED ANIMALS

Finally, let's:

Yay, we're all done!

If you don't know, now you know.

Biggy

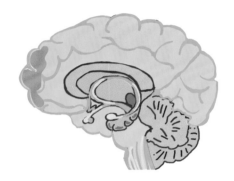

Growth Mindset
+
Executive Function Skills

These questions will garner both a growth
mindset in children and help them develop
their executive function skills.

QUESTIONS TO ASK EVERYDAY:

How can you tell?
What do you notice?
Why do you think so?
What parts do you understand?
What does it make you wonder?
Where could you look for that information?

What do you think you might need right now?

178

SCREEN TIME RECOMMENDATIONS:

*Age 2 and under: avoid media use (except video chatting).

*Preschoolers: No more than one hour of high-quality programming per day.

*Grade-schoolers and Teens: Don't let media displace other important activities such as quality sleep, regular exercise, family meals, and "unplugged" downtime.

*All ages: Be a media mentor. Co-view media with your kids.

*The American Academy of Pediatrics (AAP)

Are you always going to stick to this? Nope! Should you feel guilty about it? Nope! Sometimes (a lot of the time) the game is to just survive the moment and if a screen gets you through it, there are worse things.

Play your way.

It's hard to act really excited about something you are not into. So do what you like to do with your kids. For me, it's the zoo or museums. Maybe for you, it's art and makeup. Whatever it is, do the things you really enjoy with your kids.

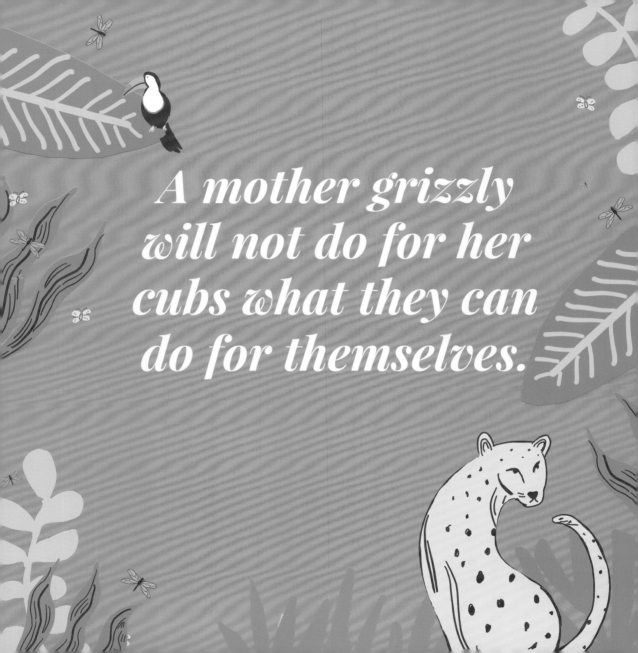

A mother grizzly will not do for her cubs what they can do for themselves.

Let them go (grow)!

Gradually give your children more and more responsibility. They can do it—I promise.

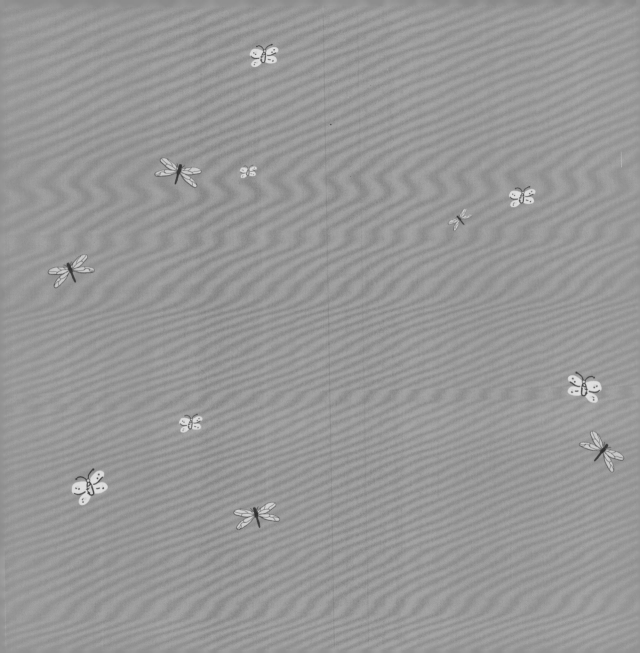

Becoming

Becoming is the process of <u>coming</u> to <u>be</u> something.

It is my sincerest hope that my children and yours are becoming their perfect authentic selves. Together, their unique abilities and talents will help heal our world, drive out hate, embrace our differences, and restore our environment. Yeah, I know it's a lot, and it is an ambitious idea. But I'm a big believer in, "trying and failing is better than not trying at all." Our children do have incredible gifts to share with the world, so how do we help them reach their full potential? I have my money on teaching them to stay strong during hard times, to practice empathy and compassion, and to be reflective of their mistakes.

No one said becoming was easy, and no one said it had to be hard either. Here are the last few skills that I have gathered that I think can help our kiddos along their journey.

Beautiful together

WHEN SOMETHING FEELS HARD:

Acknowledge big feelings.

"I get it, it can be frustrating when we learn something new."

Bring up YET.

"You can't do it—YET!"

Praise the process.

"I love how hard you are working on that." "I'm so proud of you for trying over and over."

Remind them how far they have come.

"Remember when you thought riding a scooter was hard, now look how well you can do that."

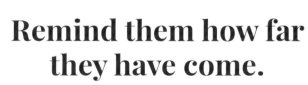

The single most common factor for children who develop resilience is at least one stable and committed relationship with a supportive parent, caregiver, or other adult.

Center on the Developing Child Harvard University

Resilience can be taught, practiced, and strengthened.

RESILIENCE TRAINING ROUTINE:

* *Practice naming and expressing feelings.*

✚

* *Practice critical thinking and persistence.*
(Basically build those executive function skills!)

✚

* *Build their confidence.*
Praise and celebrate who they are and how they are growing every day.

✚

* *Create a community of loving caring grown-ups that support your child.*

Keep connected with supportive friends, family, and organizations by attending and participating in events when you can.

✚

* *Take care of yourself.*

Take breaks when you need them and prioritize your needs. A healthy, caring grown up is the most essential part of raising a resilient child.

192

This builds confidence.

Children feel more secure when they know there are grown-ups who care about them.

Strengthens resilience.

My Super Stars

ACTIVITY

1. Draw and cut out several stars.

2. Help your child decorate the stars with photos or drawings of the grown-ups who care for them.

3. Punch holes in the stars you have decorated.

4. Loop string through the holes, and help your child hang it anywhere!

ADAPTED FROM WWW.SESAMESTREETINCOMMUNITIES.ORG

When I was a boy and I would see scary things in the news, my mother would say to me, "Look for the helpers. You will always find people who are helping."

Fred Rogers

Keeping to familiar routines can be very comforting. Choose at least one routine that you can keep every day. Simple things like extra cuddles every morning or the same lullaby every night can give kids a sense of structure and safety.

Sesame street

We rise by lifting others.

Robert G. Ingersoll

HELPING HANDS ACTIVITY

*Trace your hand and your little's hand.

TRUMAN

I help when I pick up my toys.

I help Truman brush his teeth.

Mommy

*On each finger, write one way you help each other.

*Display the hands in a place everyone can see. Before bed, look at the hands together and invite everyone to name one way they helped someone today. Try it in the morning too. Invite everyone to name one way they plan to help someone today.

198

What you are

not changing

you are

choosing.

upstander

/ˈəpˌstandər/

noun

1. A person who speaks or acts in support of an individual or cause, particularly someone who intervenes on behalf of a person being attacked or bullied.

"An upstander does what is right even when they are alone."

Oxford Dictionary

RAISING AN UPSTANDER

1. Build their confidence.

Point out specific talents and unique traits that make them so special. Celebrate their individualism and perseverance every day.

2. When you see something, say something.

Children learn so much from our modeled behavior. If they see us helping out someone or taking a positive action when something is wrong or unjust, they learn to do the same.

3. Teach them what to say when someone isn't nice or fair to them:

If someone makes a rude comment to you, you should tell them their comment is not okay.

"That was rude."

"Please stop."

"Be nice."

If someone asks a rude question, respond with pride.

"My eye shape is a shape of Chinese eyes. I love my eyes! Different shapes are beautiful!"

Walk away or get a grown-up if they don't say sorry.

4. When someone isn't nice or fair to someone else:

Help the victim get away:

"Hey, do you want to sit with us?"

Offer friendship and kindness to the victim:

"Are you ok?"

"I saw what happened, that was not cool."

Get a grown-up.

If you see someone being unkind to someone else and it's not safe to stop them, get a grown-up.

5. Teach empathy and understanding.

"When people are mean, it's normally because they are hurting inside or embarrassed."

6. Talk about events after they have happened.

"What did you do? What do you think you can do next time? It's normal to feel frozen or to want to run away, let's talk about it."

7. Remind them that there are so many kind people in this world that want to make it a better place, just like them. Look for the helpers and list all the good people in their lives and communities.

dehumanizing language
/dēˈ(h)yo͞oməˌnīziNG ˈlaNGgwij/

noun

1. Any language that is used to deny a person or group of people humanness, to characterize them as less than human.

"In a range of studies, psychologists have been able to show how dehumanizing messages can influence how we think about and treat people."—Allison Skinner

Look back at some of the most tragic episodes in human history, and you will find words and images that stripped people of their basic human traits. In the Nazi era, the film *The Eternal Jew* depicted Jews as rats. During the Rwandan genocide, Hutu officials called Tutsis "cockroaches" that needed to be cleared out.

Brian Resnick

When we take a moment to separate the act, the condition, or the circumstance from the person, we make room to see that person more wholly.

SUBTLE WAYS TO HUMANIZE MORE:

INSTEAD OF THIS :	**TRY THIS:**
"That's a homeless person."	"That's a person that doesn't have a home right now."
"She is mean."	"She said a mean thing. She's probably having a bad day."
"He is a criminal."	"He is a person that committed a crime."

206

Never allow dehumanization in our language or in our children's language.

Dr. Aliza Pressman

To show up
imperfectly but
open to change, is
better than not
showing up at all.

Stephanie Dixon

The beauty of anti-racism is that you don't have to pretend to be free of racism to be an anti-racist. Anti-racism is the commitment to fight racism wherever you find it, including in yourself. And it's the only way forward.

Ijeoma Oluo

CELEBRATE DIVERSITY!

Our children have powerful natural observation skills. When they notice a difference in skin color, eye or nose shape, talk about it!

If we shy away from conversations about race our kids might think it's something they shouldn't talk about too.

210

The heartbeat of racism is denial.

Ibram X. Kendi

implicit bias

/imˈplisit ˈbīəs/

noun

1. A preference or aversion to a group of people that we are unaware of.

"Once you are aware of your implicit bias, you can make an effort to adjust your thoughts and actions."

Did you know you can take an online quiz to discover your implicit bias?

Make it an ongoing conversation.

owth never endsGrowth never ne

th never ends Growth never ends Growth ne

Growth never ends Growth nev

Growth never ends

214

Three steps forward and two
steps back *is* progress.

People hurt people when they are hurting.

(This is why junior high is so traumatic.)

HOW TO GROW
Compassion

Like all muscles, compassion can grow and become stronger, or it can atrophy. Here are three ways to grow that muscle:

1 First, and always first, offer yourself compassion.
Scan your circumstances. Have you not slept well in months because of a toddler hijacking your bed each night at 2 a.m.? Are you hungry? Has a colleague been parking in YOUR parking spot, and you're pretty sure it has been intentional? Whatever it is, take a breath and offer yourself compassion in this moment. Think to yourself, "I love you as you are, and I'm sorry you are suffering."

2 Expand your awareness of connection.
While driving, consider the road, consider the people who worked to build it, think of the people who built the machines, and consider the people who made the materials. Imagine all the people who worked so that you could drive on this road. This practice can be done anytime: in line at the grocery store, in your kitchen as you make lunch, or wherever you may be. There is so much interconnection when we take a moment to consider it.

3 Grow kindness and empathy through meditation and journaling.
Try the meditation on the next page, or explore the many guided meditations and activities available online at sites like Greater Good in Action (GGIA.Berkeley.edu).

CIRCLES OF COMPASSION

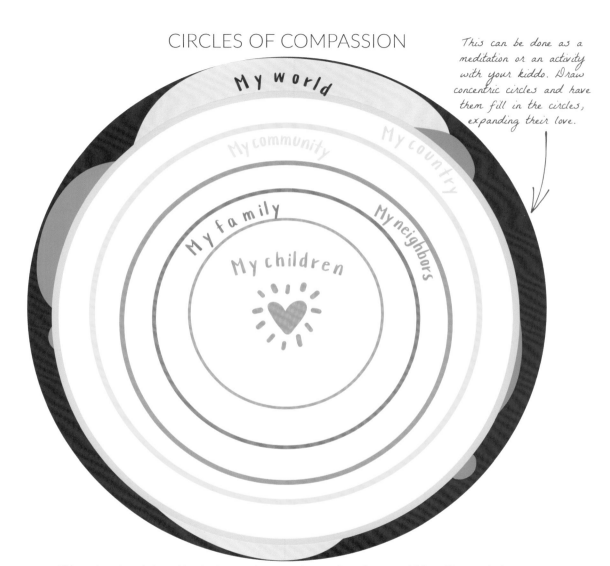

My world

My community

My country

My family

My neighbors

My children

This can be done as a meditation or an activity with your kiddo. Draw concentric circles and have them fill in the circles, expanding their love.

Take a deep breath in and let the love and compassion you have for your children fill your whole body. On the next inhale imagine expanding that compassion to your other family members, exhale. On the next inhale offer that compassion to your neighbors. And so on and so on until you feel compassion for our whole world.

There are no right or wrong ways to be a family.

99.9% of people are really good people.

MY GRANDPA

You are never
too small to
make a
difference.

One large tree
=
A day's worth of oxygen for four people.

The earth is what we all have in common.

Wendell Berry

SIMPLE WAYS TO TEACH YOUR KIDS
TO CARE FOR THE EARTH:

* Pick up trash together.

    * Make upcycled arts and crafts together.

       * Garden together.

Teaches them about
healthy food and
connects them with nature.

*Visit zoos and aquariums
to learn about endangered
species and habitats.

224

I'm proud of you, I love the person you are becoming, and I'm always here for you.

Say this a lot. Say it to your kids, to yourself, your spouse—whoever needs it.

The greatest thing you'll ever learn is
just to love and be loved in return.
Eden Ahbez

American Academy of Pediatrics

Healthychildren.org

Powered by 67,000 pediatricians, this website covers a huge range of topics including screen time, gender identity, and Autism Spectrum Disorder.

Anti-Defamation League

ADL.org

The leading anti-hate organization with tons of resources for parents and educators.

Center on the Developing Child Harvard University

Developingchild.harvard.edu

Get a deep dive into the inner workings of a child's brain.

Sesame Street in Communities

Sesamestreetincommunities.org

So many amazing activities and videos that help both parents and children get through whatever life throws at them.

Understood

Understood.org

Great resources for people who learn or think differently.

This book is dedicated to the three perfect tiny humans in my life: Truman, Hendrik, and Escher. I love you infinity times around the multiverse and I am so so grateful to be your mom. Code 4,37.

About the Author

LIZ SWENSON

is a mom to three and a high school math teacher with a Master of Science in Mathematics. She is the author and illustrator of *You Got This, Mama! From Boobs to Blowouts a Survival Guide for New Moms.* Liz lives in sunny San Clemente, California with her husband and three perfect children.

230

LizSwenson.org
Facebook.com/LizSwensonbff
Instagram.com/LizSwensonbff

About Familius

Visit Our Website: www.familius.com

Familius is a global trade publishing company that publishes books and other content to help families be happy. We believe that happy families are key to a better society and the foundation of a happy life. The greatest work anyone will ever do will be within the walls of his or her own home. And we don't mean vacuuming! We recognize that every family looks different and passionately believe in helping all families find greater joy, whatever their situation. To that end, we publish beautiful books that help families live our 10 Habits of Happy Family Life: love together, play together, learn together, work together, talk together, heal together, read together, eat together, give together, and laugh together. Further, Familius does not discriminate on the basis of race, color, religion, gender, age, nationality, disability, caste, or sexual orientation in any of its activities or operations. Founded in 2012, Familius is located in Sanger, California.

Connect
Facebook: www.facebook.com/familiusbooks
Pinterest: www.pinterest.com/familiusbooks
Instagram: @FamiliusBooks
TikTok: @FamiliusBooks

FAMILIUS

"The most important work you ever do will be within the walls of your own home."

Copyright © 2024 by Liz Swenson
All rights reserved.

Published by Familius LLC, www.familius.com
PO Box 1249, Reedley, CA 93654

Familius books are available at special discounts for bulk purchases, whether for sales promotions or for family or corporate use. For more information, contact Familius Sales at orders@familius.com.

Reproduction of this book in any manner, in whole or in part, without written permission of the publisher is prohibited.

Library of Congress Control Number: 2023948588

Print ISBN 9781641707558

EPUB ISBN 9781641708531

Kindle ISBN 9781641708524

Fixed PDF ISBN 9781641708517

Printed in China

Edited by Michele Robbins
Sensitivity review by Lwazi Vazhure
Cover design by Carlos Mireles-Guerrero

Book design by Liz Swenson

10 9 8 7 6 5 4

First Edition